www.poetryforfunerals.com

Poetry for FUNERALS

*... such lovely words. You captured everything about Mum
beautifully. I will cherish this poem forever. Thank you...*

*... You made Dad's service all the more special with that beautiful poem.
Absolutely him in a nutshell! You are both a Godsend...*

Poetry for FUNERALS

by Kate Armon and Craig Smith

Poetry for Funerals

By Kate Armon and Craig Smith

Published by CK Publishing

armonandsmithcelebrants@gmail.com

©2023 CK Publishing

Editor: Craig Smith
Designer: CK Publishing
Cover Image: Craig Smith

for all the families we have had the privilege of helping

Acknowledgements

This book would not have been written if it wasn't for the incredible kindness and encouragement shown by several people.

Firstly, thank you to Brian and June Armon for their continued support and belief in our work and its value. To Aaron and Kerrie Burkin from Beaudesert Funerals for giving us early opportunities to shine. To Karen Lucas and Julie Kat at Artisan Funerals, who have supported our poetry from the very start. And to Tim and Gina Connolly and their team at Newhaven Funerals for their ongoing encouragement and for giving us the honour of working with them.

To our four children, Nathan, Kane, Charlotte and Rosie, who constantly provide us with precious support and inspiration for everything we do.

And lastly, to all our friends and colleagues worldwide who have backed us in this endeavour and given us the belief in ourselves that we were on the right path.

Thank you, one and all.

Kate and Craig x

Contents

Contents

About the Authors

Kate and Craig are a husband-and-wife team of funeral celebrants living on the beautiful Gold Coast in Australia. Originally from the UK, Kate and her family have always been a little nomadic, spending 15 years in New Zealand before moving downunder. There, she fell in love with Craig before finally settling down.

Craig is originally from Melbourne but moved to the Gold Coast for the weather and family. Between them, they have four beautiful children, and family life is at the centre of everything they do. They both adore the Gold Coast and cannot imagine living anywhere else in the world.

Kate started out as a wedding celebrant in New Zealand. Being a celebrant for funerals was not something she thought she would have the emotional strength to pursue. But, on her mum's insistence, Kate finally took her first funeral. Fifteen years later, she is a dedicated funeral celebrant, and she can't imagine doing anything else with her life. Being a funeral celebrant is a passion for her.

Craig had spent his life working in video production but was also an accomplished actor. When he met and married Kate, it became obvious to her that he was an incredibly talented individual. He was a man of integrity, compassion and empathy, all the attributes he needed to be a funeral celebrant. It wasn't easy to convince him however, and it took some months of persuasion and finally convincing him to stand up at a funeral to read a poem. He was a natural in every way possible. Not only a confident public speaker but a man that families just fell in love with.

It was a match made in heaven, Kate and Craig bring something unique to their roles as husband and wife funeral celebrants. They believe that two hearts are stronger than one and that together they offer a far more comprehensive service to their families. Making a connection with families is one of their strongest qualities, and it was this connection that led them into the world of poetry writing.

Why this Book?

As Funeral Celebrants, we often find the need to use poetry in our services. And while there are hundreds of well-established poems out there by some fantastic authors, we found that we were looking for something that was far more specific to the loved one of the family we were looking after.

> *"A poem is such a lovely thing,*
>
> *with all the comfort it can bring..."*

While poems like, *Look for Me in Rainbows* by Vicky Brown and *She is Gone* by David Harkins are truly wonderful poems and perfectly acceptable for any funeral service and will continue to be so, the need for bespoke poetry that would uniquely reflect the individual became clear.

Our experience with poetry was limited. Having a theatre background and a love of Shakespeare, I could see the beauty of a poetic verse, but my experience in writing it had not extended to anything beyond Year 12 English! As for Craig, poetry to him meant things like *the boy stood on the burning deck*, and anything that rhymed with the word *Venus*! Oh yes, my husband is ever the child! But it was during one particular family meeting that the idea of writing our own poetry was ignited.

We had gone to see the husband of a beautiful lady who had, tragically, succumbed to breast cancer. She was only in her forties and had such a passion for life. As we sat and listened to her story, we were particularly moved by the sheer inner strength this lady possessed, to fight such a hard battle, and keep her family motivated and protected for the inevitability of what was to come.

She had a great love for animals, and their home was shared with horses, goats, chickens, cats and dogs, all of whom loved her dearly. Each morning, despite her pain and discomfort, she would rise at the crack of dawn to feed them all and look after their needs. She always put others before herself and it was impossible not to be consumed by the enormous sense of loss of her passing.

We discussed readings and verses with her husband, and as we sifted through our vast collection of poems, there was nothing that jumped out as being absolutely right for the service. Sure, there were poems that describe the loss we feel and verses that portray everyone's best wishes for those who have passed, but there was nothing that really captured the essence of who this lovely lady was. Without thinking, we found ourselves offering to write something unique for the day!

As we made the hour-long journey home, we sat in silence, each wondering what we had done. We both considered ourselves pretty good writers - we can certainly write a heck of a good service - but neither of us had ever turned our hands to poetry. Over the next twenty-four hours we sat staring at a blank page, we dragged the whiteboard out, we threw sentences around, shuffled words and experimented with rhyme, all trying to capture the essence of who this lady was.

We grounded the poem around her love of animals and used that as a metaphor for her love of life and family. It was an incredibly personal and cathartic process to complete, and when we delivered it on the day of the service, her husband sat in tears as we read it to the crowd of fifty or so. As we gave him a framed copy, he hugged us and told us he couldn't have asked for anything better as a tribute to his beautiful wife.

Some may see that first poem as a little simplistic, our others have matured in style since then, but we felt it was so important to include it as part of this collection. Since then, we have gone on to write many personalised poems for some of the lovely families we have had the privilege of helping.

Writing poetry has become a part of who we are as celebrants. And although we do not write a poem for every funeral we officiate, we do write when it is called for, either when what we are looking for simply cannot be found or when something extraordinary about the person touches our hearts.

Our poems, we are proud to say, have found their way all over the world. We often get contacted by other celebrants and families, asking if they can use one of our poems in their services. We feel honoured that people want to use our poetry at services and privileged to know that they give families some sense of comfort in what is their hardest time.

This book is for celebrants, officiants and families looking for something a little different.

How to Get the Best From This Book

The poems in this book are free to use at funeral or memorial services. All we ask is that you acknowledge us as the original authors.

Each poem is introduced with a short background to the poem and for whom it was inspired. Under the description opposite each poem, you will see a section called *Tips to Customise.* In most cases, each poem can be customised to some degree.

Tips to Customise

This section will give you some handy tips on how to customise the poem.

These tips will provide customisation suggestions. For instance, male can be changed to female, or any locations mentioned can be adjusted to regionalise the poem. There are a couple of poems within the book where we have two variations on a theme. For instance, *The Vegetable Gardener* and *The Flower Gardener* are, in essence, the same poem but with verses that have been altered to suit. These are prime examples of how a poem can be uniquely customised to suit a funeral.

Some poems in this book have been created to be very specific to a particular person. As you read, you may find that some verses may not suit or be appropriate to that person. In this case, the tips may suggest you drop or change the verse as needed.

Poems, like *Always There*, *The Jigsaw* and *Each Day I Wake*, have a more generic feel, and we hope that these poems will still be read at funerals for many years to come.

A funeral poem may be warm and tender, like *The Jigsaw*, or humorous, like *Keep the Tinnies Cold*. Whichever poem you choose, just make sure it matches the tone you set for the funeral in accordance with your family's wishes.

If you are a celebrant or a family member and would like us to write a poem for a loved one, please drop us an email at poetry4funerals@gmail.com, we would be happy to assist.

We sincerely hope you enjoy these poems .

Kate and Craig x

Part 1

FUNERAL POEMS

The Jigsaw
In memory of Elizabeth

We were approached by a gentleman from a small country town, some three hours from where we lived, to officiate his mother's funeral. As we chatted with him, it became clear that this lovely lady was truly the heart of this family. In his eulogy, which he had sent us a couple of days prior to the service, he spoke of his family as a giant jigsaw puzzle that fit together tightly. This one line gave us the inspiration to write *The Jigsaw*.

Tips to Customise

This gender of this poem can easily be changed from Mother to Father.

The reference in the last verse can be changed to a specific name if suitable.

The Jigsaw

by Kate Armon and Craig Smith

When I was young, my mother bought
A jigsaw just for me.
Many pieces to make a picture of
Our unique family tree.

I dumped the pieces on the top,
they scattered far and wide.
"Here's a tip", my mother said,
"Always start along the sides."

Across the years, the puzzle grew,
From segments to a whole.
Our little family tree was formed,
Joined as just one soul.

All the shapes that made that whole,
I'd stare at them in awe.
Our family pieces fit together,
And made up our Jigsaw.

Stronger when the pieces bond,
With edges flush and true.
Our picture was one of family,
The heart of it was you.

The puzzle finished but the picture changed,
As every season came.
Our pieces fit so perfectly,
Our heartbeat was the same.

The Jigsaw sits there on the top,
But now a different view.
I see your outline in the empty space,
Of the piece that once was you.

Thank you, Mum for all you've left,
Your legacy and more.
'Cause in our minds you'll always be,
The heart of our Jigsaw.

Those Boots to Fill

In memory of Vince

This poem was written for a gentlemen whose whole life was spent around horses. A hard worker, he was up at the crack of dawn and spent many years as a race horse trainer. Told from the perspective of a child looking back upon memories and realising a lot to live up to, this poem is perfect for any man with a love of horses.

Tips to Customise

Verse four can be removed if not appropriate to your family. The last verse mentions a doorstep, this was in reference to the daughter's memories of always seeing her Dad's boots on the back doorstep. This line could be altered to – "*In my mind I'll form that picture clear*".

Those Boots to Fill

by Kate Armon and Craig Smith

When the sun's first rays, creep across the yard,
And my breath snaps upon the chill.
You're already there in the mists of morn,
And there's those boots to fill.

A gentle man, so fit and strong,
You were never one to boast.
Just working hard, from day to day,
For those you loved the most.

A guiding hand to each and all,
You taught us all to ride.
Up in the saddle, high and tall,
Your family was your pride.

And in the silks the furlongs cross,
With the pounding of the hooves.
With reins in hand, a trainer's brand,
Your skill was ne'er disproved.

Now, in some time of calm reflect,
Through a veil of childlike eyes.
I'll see you there in shadowed glare,
Framed in that sunrise.

For to me, you were a hero then,
And more, for all those years.
And now each time I close my eyes,
Your memory appears.

The reins hang there upon the hook,
The bits and bridles too.
The stables stay alive with love,
And our memories of you.

When I look upon my own time here,
And some days, I'm sure I will.
In my mind I'll picture that doorstep clear,
And see those boots to fill.

The Fisherman
In memory of Martin

Sometimes you meet a family that truly touches your heart. The stories they share can resonate with you in profound ways. The gentleman this poem was written for had a deep love for fishing, he loved the serenity of being out on the open waves, with a few rods set up. He shared his passion with his son at an early age and the two of them would spend hours together, on their boat.

He also had a love for music and was quite an accomplished pianist. His strong sense of family and the pride he had in his children were very clear. We wrote this poem from the perspective of the child reminiscing about his father.

Tips to Customise

This poem would be suitable for man with a love of fishing. If the person was not musical at all, the fifth verse could be removed.

This poem was written in a similar cadence to Banjo Patterson's *Clancy of the Overflow* and should be read in the same fashion.

The Fisherman

by Craig Smith and Kate Armon

As I watched him cast a line, I find my memories of that time
Are clouded deep within my feelings for the days long past and won.
This able-bodied man, with his olive sun-kissed tan,
I couldn't help but stare in awe, for he was "The Fisherman."

He would sit there patiently waiting, for the fish that he was baiting,
Just for a bite or nibble that would feed his family fair.
And through the ocean spray so splendid, this little boat that he had tendered
Bobbed up and down across the waves amongst the salty air.

He was at home upon the ocean, with its gentle rocking motion
And the silence of his thoughts brought forth memories to remind.
For his family made him strong, they were his soulful inner song
And nothing can break the bond of a heart that's so entwined.

And the things that made him glad, as a husband and a dad,
Were the times he always cherished with his family by his side
For the joy that they did bring, did truly make him sing,
And the things that they accomplished filled his heart with so much pride.

And the songs from all those years, go ringing in my ears,
As his fingers danced across the well-worn keys both black and white.
And I'm sure that he was wishing, both piano and his fishing
Could be one as both together in an ever-wondrous sight.

And the respect from one and all, was something that could never fall
For he was a man of honour as sure as day is long.
And the love across their sleeve makes it harder when they grieve
The loss of such a man whose heart was both as tender as was strong.

And as the sun sets on the bow, he can rightly claim of how
He had the best that life can bring, when all is said and done.
With my praise for him eternal, as I write this in my journal
Yes, I'm proud to say I loved him, for he was My Fisherman.

I Hope There's A Hen House In Heaven

In memory of Roger

Not all funeral poetry has to be sad. Often we meet with families who are looking for something lighter, even though their grief is just as real.

We come across so many animal lovers on our travels. This lovely man adored his hens, he called them his 'girls'. He loved spending time tending to them, feeding them or just sitting watching them scratch around searching for seed, it was the most peaceful part of his day.

So, in honour of Roger, we just had to write a poem about his chooks.

Tips to Customise

The breed of chickens can be changed to suit.
eg.

> *'There's Leghorns and Cochins and Barnvelders too,*
> *Welsummers, Polands and Reds.'*

Or any other combination that would suit. The Breed, *'Reds'* needs to remain as to maintain the imperfect rhyme with 'eggs'.

I Hope There's A Hen House In Heaven

by Craig Smith and Kate Armon

I hope there's a hen house in heaven
Where I can sit and watch them all day.
I'll watch them all feed as I throw out some seed
And let them all scratch in the hay.

That happy old sound in the morning
When the sun shares its light for the day.
The cluck of their song as they wander along
And the hens all come out for a play

There's Bantams and Silkies and Australorps too,
Orpingtons, Plymouths and Reds.
Each chook with a name, all flighty and game,
And my, all those wonderful eggs!

The calm they all give me is peaceful
I simply can't put into words.
My lovely young hens just play in their pens
They're more than just wonderful birds.

I'll sit as the hours go fleeting away
Watching the colour fade out from the skies.
When the time is just right, they'll go in for the night
And all say their nightly goodbyes.

So, I hope there's a hen house in heaven,
With an endless amount of some grain.
Yes, I'll feed them all day as the scratch and they play
'Til the time when we'll all meet again

Alone

As funeral celebrants we spend a great deal of our life surrounded by other's loss and grief. We do our best to maintain our professionalism at services but sometime our own emotions get the better of us. This usually happens in the car on the way home as we discuss how the service went.

When we write poetry for others this same emotional reaction occurs and we put ourselves into their places and wonder how we would feel if it was one of us who had died.

They say writing is cathartic and a good counselor, *'Alone'* was written from our own perspective and imagining our own feelings towards the loss of each other.

Tips to Customise

This poem is of a more generic nature and, as such, has no customisation options.

Alone

by Craig Smith and Kate Armon

As I watch the sunset from your chair,
I find a single strand of hair,
My heart it breaks without you here,
The emptiness, the feel of fear.

Our lives entwined, and ne'er apart,
We were as one right from the start,
But the price is high for all that love,
Now I'm here and you're above.

To sleep without your arms around me,
To wake and know you've gone without me,
My days are empty, my heart is broken,
Trying to hold on to our last words spoken.

My heart is numb, I call your name,
I know my life won't be the same,
I close my eyes to see your face,
But silence falls upon this place.

Now what to do, where do I go?
I'm lost like a child in a blizzard of snow,
I call out your name, the quiet so loud,
But nothing returns, a lonely shroud.

I feel so helpless now you're gone,
But I know you'd want me to go on.
I know your love will see me through,
Until the day that I'm with you.

So, when that day comes around and then,
When I can smile at you again.
I'll know that when my time is done,
Our souls again will be as one.

The Vegetable Gardener
In memory of Jimmy

This poem was originally simply titled as, 'The Gardener', and was written for an elderly gentleman who loved his garden and had established quite a significant vegetable patch! As we sat with his family, they described the passion he had for his little vegetable garden and all the varieties of vegetables he had grown over the years.

A wonderful provider and a sturdy father with a strict moral code, his passion for gardening was used as an analogy for raising his children and looking after his family.

Tips to Customise

The subject can be easily changed from Male to Female to suit.

The names of the gardener as well as the various plants could also be changed to suit the person.

If the gender is changed to female, Line Four of Verse Six can be changed to *'from worries (trouble) and from strife'*

Customisation Example:

A principal from an Elementary School in Iowa, Michelle Cole, wrote to us and asked if she could adapt this poem for one of her teachers, who taught in her school for 30 years. This is how she adapted a couple of our verses.

A lifetime spent in classrooms,
Planting all the seeds,
Providing for each student,
Just what their little hearts need.

Students grew in great abundance,
College ready and future bright,
She cared for them most tenderly,
She cared all day and night.

The Vegetable Gardener

by Kate Armon and Craig Smith

Trowel in hand he stood there proud,
Of Tomatoes that he'd sown.
Of Courgettes, Carrots, Beans and Herbs,
All of which he'd grown.

A lifetime spent with earthy hands,
From planting all the seed.
Providing for his family,
A feast from which to feed.

Veggies grew in great abundance,
Of every colour bright.
He cared for them most tenderly,
He cared both day and night.

Patiently he tended
To all his little sprouts,
Watering and nurturing,
With a love that saw no droughts.

Always proud but often strict,
This gardener had a way.
Of helping little seedlings grow,
So none would ever stray.

Jimmy loved his garden,
His veggies were his life.
It was also somewhere to escape,
When in trouble with his wife.

So, think of him next time you stand,
Where a pretty garden grows.
For there he'll be in sun and earth,
And in the wind that blows.

The Flower Gardener
In memory of Phyllis

This is a good example of how the poems can be altered to suit your needs, as this one was adapted from the previous, *"The Vegetable Gardener"*.

We went to visit this lady's family in the nursing home where she had spent the last few years of her life. They were packing up her things into boxes, sorting out what to be kept and what could go to charity. Each item bore a distinct memory. We stepped out of her room, onto her little patio and the small garden she so tirelessly maintained. The small space was full of Bromeliads and Cordylines, her favourites, a festival of colour and beauty, so carefully tended and looked after.

Like the poem *'The Veggie Gardener'*, we used flowers as an analogy for raising her children and looking after her family.

Tips to Customise

The subject can be easily changed from Female to Male to suit.

In Verse Six, the names of the gardener can be changed to suit.

The plant names could also be changed to suit the person.
eg. *'Of Rambling Rose and Hollyhocks'*

The Flower Gardener

by Kate Armon and Craig Smith

Trowel in hand she stood there proud,
Of flowers that she'd grown,
Of Bromeliads and Cordylines,
All of which she'd sown.

A lifetime spent with earthy hands,
From planting all the seed,
The anchor of her family,
The one they all did need.

Flowers grew in every corner,
Not a patch of earth was seen,
Every inch of blooming colour,
A sign of where she'd been.

Patiently she tended,
To all her little sprouts,
Watering and nurturing,
A good Mother there, no doubts.

Always proud and full of love,
This gardener had a way
Of helping little seedlings grow
So none would ever stray.

Phyllis cherished her little garden,
But missed her one true love,
They'll both be gardening together now,
In a little patch above.

So, think of her next time you stand,
Where a flower garden grows,
For there she'll be in sun and earth,
And in the wind that blows.

The House That Wally Built

In memory of Wally

A family who we fell in love with the moment we met them. We sat with them and enjoyed tea in a proper cup and saucer on the verandah of the house that Wally built. His loss was a huge shock to his family after a tragic accident, and their grief was very raw. They opened their hearts to us and it was one of the most beautiful services we have ever had the privilege to perform. As we sat in Wally's house and heard the stories of how he laid every brick, and banged every nail and carved every wooden corbel, the poem started to form.

Tips to Customise

This poem would be suitable for someone who built their own house and was good with their hands.

The name can be changed to suit. If they do not have children verse four can be omitted.

16

The House That Wally Built

by Kate Armon and Craig Smith

Amongst the birds and trees of green,
A canvas of soil and silt.
A plan came forth, a picture seen,
Of the House that Wally built.

Foundations laid and tools in hand,
The shed was first to rise.
Weekends worked till darkness fell,
Wiping sawdust from his eyes.

With hands of steel, he laid the beams,
For strength, and paint for show.
With care and pride in every touch,
This home began to grow.

And as it grew in taking shape,
Little helpers joined the fight.
Lift it up and push it over,
A bit more to the right!

This adventure was his pride and joy,
From first nail to the last.
In every stroke and every joint,
A guiding hand did pass.

And when his dream had borne its fruit,
On everything that he'd grown.
His respect and love was guaranteed,
To reap all that he'd sown.

So, break out the china and warm the pot,
For his favourite time of day.
A time to share, a time to care,
This was the Wally way.

The shed sits quiet, the tools laid down,
But forever we'll hear the lilt.
Of the man whose soul will always be
In the House that Wally built.

The Campers
In memory of Lawrence

Losing a partner, especially one who has formed such an integral part of your life is never easy. Inseparable from the moment they met, this beautiful couple loved the outdoors and enjoyed nothing more than packing up the Campervan and taking off on holiday. A meticulous planner, when it came to camping he would prefer to let the prevailing winds lay and they would set off on an adventure.

Tips to Customise

This poem was written in a similar cadence to Banjo Patterson's *Clancy of the Overflow* and should be read in the same fashion.

This poem would be suitable for a couple with a love of camping. If you feel that the poem is too long, verses Four or Six could be omitted.

The Campers

by Craig Smith and Kate Armon

With the rise of early morn, and through the chilly breath of dawn,
The Campers stand there waiting eagerly for the next trip to begin.
Locking down their faithful load, looking forward to the road,
Open spaces were their playground, two travelling hearts akin.

When the morning sun grows brighter, the campers find their hearts grow lighter,
As the roadways and the highways open up their prospects true.
Passing hills of green and gold, these nomadic days of old,
Saw each stop a new experience, each place a different view.

Without a plan the couple steered, 'til the camping spot appeared,
Such was the ease of life a travelling and the freedom of the road.
To their next great destination, anywhere across the nation,
For the camper has no pace to keep, no burden to unload.

And when the sun sets on the day, with ribbons long of pink and grey,
The campers sit there quietly musing of adventures yet to come.
While the billy keeps a boiling, and the campers keep on toiling,
In the parks and in the lay-by's where the lonely rivers run.

And their memories never tire, sharing stories around the fire,
Bringing smiles to all the faces in the flicker of the glow.
And the sounds of nature's splendour, singing gently, soft and tender,
In the darkness brings the warmth of the camper's hearts on show.

Under skies of coloured streamers, sat this lovely pair of dreamers,
Thinking of the road ahead and more adventures on their way.
Beneath stars that twinkled brightly, they slept so sound and tightly,
And rose with birds a singing, with each dawn, a brand-new day.

And they'll travel on and ever, these two hearts that ne'er shall sever
With the rain upon their faces, and the grass beneath their feet.
Across the long and lonely highways, down the dusty roads and byways,
Sees the campers go a trav'lin to the march of their own beat.

And the stars will tell us stories, of the camper's tales of glories,
Through the cities and the bush and ever where their wheels did roam.
But there comes a time to cease, and now the camper's soul's at peace,
Just one last road to travel, as the camper journeys home.

Look up to the Sky
In memory of Joyce

Written for a Mum who was a real character. Her favourite times were the yearly cruise holidays with her daughter. She loved any chance to be the star of the show and needed no encouragement to get up on stage or perform karaoke. Centre stage and centre of attention was where this lady belonged, and she brought a lot of joy to those around her.

This poem is suitable for an outgoing and gregarious person who loves cruising and joining in with everything on board.

Tips to Customise

If a singer, but not a dancer, Verse One, line Four can be changed to:
'Remember me singing, the star of the show.'

To change the perspective from a daughter to a son, Verse Three, lines Three and Four can be changed to:
*'Cruising on ships, the laughter in tonnes
With you by my side, the best of sons.'*

And the last two lines of Verse Six can be changed to:
*'Happy and peaceful my work here is done,
Goodbye to you now, my beautiful son.'*

Look up to the Sky

by Kate Armon and Craig Smith

Please don't sit in a darkened room,
With tear-stained cheeks so full of gloom,
Instead, be jolly and let me go,
Remember me dancing, the star of the show.

I loved the fun, the frolics of life
Not the misery, heartaches or dealing with strife,
Try to remember how we loved good laughs,
Look back with fond memories at photographs.

I loved all our holidays spent together,
It didn't matter where we went or even the weather,
Cruising on ships across the waters,
We took over the boat, you were the best of daughters.

Remember me crooning as I sang with my friends,
On nights that we wished would have no ends,
I don't want to look down and see you cry,
But instead, smile and look up to the sky.

Love me and miss me but let me go,
It's time now for you to live your life and grow,
If not for yourself then do it for me,
Look after yourself and be who you want to be.

Next time you're sailing raise a glass to me,
And know that I'm there a part of the sea,
Happy and peaceful at one with the water,
Goodbye to you now, my beautiful daughter.

Each Day I Wake

Every now and then Craig and I will write a poem that isn't for anyone in particular but might be the result of a funeral we have shared together. We come home feeling the weight of grief from the family we have helped and we feel the need to sit down and write together about how we feel.

This is especially true when we recognise our own lives in others and you can't help but put yourselves in their place, and you ask yourself the question; "How would I feel?"

Tips to Customise

This poem is of a more generic nature and, as such, has no customisation options.

Each Day I Wake

by Craig Smith and Kate Armon

Each day I wake and wonder,
If today you will be there,
But with morning rise tears fill my eyes,
And I find that you're nowhere.

Just another day without you,
One more to walk alone.
The sight of you fades from my view,
And I'm once more on my own.

Your scent fades from the pillow,
As time slowly marches on.
Your clothes still hang there on the rack,
Your essence all but gone.

They say that I must set you free,
But just how could they know?
As the seasons pass without you here,
I dare not let you go.

For the memory of you calms me,
And gives me peace of mind,
To know we'll be together again,
Our hearts and souls entwined.

So, when I wake and wonder,
And my eyes begin to tear.
I'll just pull through and think of you,
And wish that you were here.

Her Last Encore
In memory of Hilda

As well as being celebrants and writers, we both have a love of the theatre. Whether that's on stage or watching. *'Her Last Encore'* was truly written from our hearts as actors. We understand the love of the stage, the smell of the grease paint and leaving an audience wanting more. This lovely woman had been involved in amateur dramatics all her life. It was her only hobby and she was passionate about it. The service was full of show tunes and it seemed only right to pen an actor's poem for her.

Tips to Customise

This gender of this poem can easily be changed from Female to Male.

She can be changed to *He*, and the Verse One reference to *actress* can be changed to *actor*.

Her Last Encore

by Kate Armon and Craig Smith

As the curtains fall,
And the lights start to fade,
An actress stands silently
Upon her last stage.

The smell of the grease paint,
The friends and the fun.
Waiting in the wings,
The overture's begun.

Nervously waiting
To tread the boards,
She runs through her lines
And sings through her chords,

The music runs through
Her soul like a friend.
It's a passion that stays with her,
Right to the end.

The roles, the songs,
The joys of it all.
Such vivid fond memories
In the actor's great hall.

The music has stopped now,
And she sings here no more,
A new journey awaits her,
Her Last Encore.

Are there Golf Courses in Heaven?
In memory of Olive

As we sat with the daughter of this lovely lady, she told us of her mother's involvement with golf, which came later in life, and her passion for it. For her, Golf was everything. She lived and breathed the game and was a significant member of the local golf club for over thirty years. She had been an active advocate for junior golf and was one of the initial mentors to Australian golfer, Jason Day.

Her faith was an important part of her life and in conversation, we all quipped that she would be up there right now improving her handicap. From that, this little poem was born.

Tips to Customise

To change the gender of the poem from male to female, Verse One, Line One can be changed to:

"And a challenging golfer's tee."

Or

'And a challenging gentleman's tee.'

The last verse for a male can be changed to:

"So think of me next time you see,
A golfer in full swing,
For there I'll be in heaven playing,
The ultimate Golfing King!"

Are there Golf Courses in Heaven?

by Kate Armon and Craig Smith

Are there golf courses in Heaven?
Beautiful greens set aside for me?
Bright sunshine and cool breezes
And a challenging ladies' tee.

I hope there's a round just waiting,
A missing player to come and play,
We can have a game, then rest together,
As we come to the end of each day.

I can be who I used to be,
Full of energy and life,
No longer hindered by earthly worries,
And constrained by illness or strife.

So, think of me next time you see,
A golf course lush and green,
For there, I'll be, in heaven playing,
The ultimate golfing Queen!

Are there Bowling Greens in Heaven?

Not written specifically for one of our families, this is another example of how one poem can be changed to reflect another theme.

Tips to Customise

To change the gender from male to female, Verse Four can be changed to:

"So, think of me next time you see,
A well-kept lawn in Spring,
For there, I'll be, in heaven playing,
The ultimate Bowling King!"

Are there Bowling Greens in Heaven?

by Kate Armon and Craig Smith

Are there bowling greens in Heaven?
Beautiful greens set aside for me?
Bright sunshine and cool breezes
And maybe a nice G & T.

I hope there's a team just waiting,
A new player to come and play,
We can have a game, then rest together,
As we come to the end of each day.

I can be who I always used to be,
Full of energy and life,
No longer hindered by earthly worries,
And constrained by illness or strife.

So, think of me next time you see,
A bowling lawn lush and green,
For there, I'll be in heaven playing,
The ultimate bowling Queen!

Always There
In memory of Maureen

The sudden loss of a loved one is difficult to come to terms with. *"Always There"* was written for a family who lost their mother suddenly to a heart attack. A very giving woman, she was always ready to lend a hand to anyone in need, and was a vital member of her community.

Her faith was an important part of her life and so, we felt, that aspect was just as important to include in verse. Just as she was always there for her family, we felt that was an obvious title.

Tips to Customise

The "Jelly Beans" reference in Verse Five was a personal one, specific to this lovely lady and could easily be customised to suit your family. eg.

> *'the jar of nuts are gone.'*

or

> *'the licorice is gone'*

Gender is not specific for this poem, so it could be used to suit either male or female.

Always There

by Kate Armon and Craig Smith

The day I left I shed a tear,
Much more I had to say.
More dreams to share and love to spare,
I wish I could have stayed.

The years we had were dear to me,
I've watched you grow and grow
Into the people you've become,
You mean more than you know.

Throughout my years I put others first,
I tried to do my best.
Always first to lend a hand,
So, I could pass God's test.

That day He came to carry me
In answer to His call.
I'm resting now the pain is gone,
My love is with you all.

The chair is empty, the room is bare,
The jelly beans are gone.
The laughter, love and happy times,
The memories will live on.

So, although I'm gone, I'm always there
In this special love we've known.
God love you, one and all my dears,
You'll never be alone.

The Last Ride

In memory of Don

A simple but powerful poem for those who love horses, we wrote this for a gentlemen for whom horses were a way of life. Whether that was riding them, training them or merely watching them at the track. They were an incredibly important aspect of his life.

His family told us that he woke at early dawn and would be down at the stables by the time the sun was rising. He would spend his days riding, training and teaching others about horses and passing on the incredible skills he had learned. Sadly ill health stopped him being able to be physically involved, but the family would take him down to the stables where he would sit in a chair and while away his days, amongst his beautiful four legged friends.

Tips to Customise

This poem is of a more generic nature and, as such, has no customisation options.

The Last Ride

by Kate Armon and Craig Smith

My beautiful creatures,
My friends and my love,
Such majesty and grace,
Sent from above.

You filled all my days,
With passion and pride,
I longed for the days,
You allowed me to ride.

Your beautiful mane,
Clasped tight in my hands,
As we ride over fields,
To a brave new land.

Take me with you,
Gallant steed of mine,
Let us ride on together,
'Til the end of time.

Stay with me always,
Never leave my side,
Let us travel together,
For this, my last ride.

The Knitter
In memory of Mary

This poem was written for a lovely lady whose favourite pastime was knitting.
It was one of her joys in life and something she was exceptionally talented at.

Not only would she make her own children's clothes, something they didn't always appreciate, but she would make pieces for new babies and sold a lot of what she made.

This service was especially memorable for us as it was for the mother of one or our funeral directors we regularly work with.

Tips to Customise

Admittedly, not many men knit, but should you need to change the gender of this poem, it can be done so easily.

Mother to Father, She to He, her to him, Mum to Dad. etc.

The Knitter

by Kate Armon and Craig Smith

My Mother was a knitter,
Who made all sorts of things,
She loved to knit for babies,
To see the joy it brings.

I remember when I was little,
The clack the needles made,
A sound that made me feel so safe,
Her love will never fade.

I loved to watch her knitting grow,
And wonder what it would be,
Knit one, pearl one, every row
I learned that patience was the key.

I never saw her drop a stitch,
Yet she never seemed to look,
Her fingers moved so fast and free,
As she read the pattern from the book.

I would wake up in the morning,
To see how far she'd got,
A little hat or jumper finished,
And tied up with a knot.

Every piece had so much heart,
A little of her in every knit,
What a precious memory I now have,
Of how I used to watch and sit.

As the ball of wool grew smaller,
It was time to say goodbye,
To the world's best Mum and knitter,
Till we meet again, fly high.

The Little Things

In memory of Tom

There are always the little things aren't there?   Those annoying little habits that a partner has that, for whatever reason, drive you mad. From leaving shoes laying around, to clothes on the end of the bed, to not putting cups in the dishwasher. Every couple has them.

In our conversations with families, we often ask, "What will you miss the most about...?'   One lovely lady who had just lost her husband of forty-six years, reeled off a whole list of little things that used to drive her crazy about him. But at the end, with tears in her eyes, she said that these were the things she would now miss on a daily basis.

On our drive home, we joked of the things about each other that drove us around the bend, those conversations were the inspiration for this poem.

Tips to Customise

The reference to tea in Verses Three and Six could be changed to Coffee.

Verse Three, Line Three can be changed to another spread. eg.

> *'Not screwing the lid of the vegemite down,'*

or:

> *'Not screwing the lid of the marmalade down,'*

or for our US friends:

> *'Not screwing the lid of the jelly jar down,'*

The Little Things

by Craig Smith and Kate Armon

I came home for the first time without you today,
The house felt empty and bare.
Your keys still hung on the hook in the hall,
Your coat slung over the chair.

The letters and bills with your name peeking through,
The ones you'd always avoid.
The silly things that you'd often do,
Little things that would make me annoyed.

Like leaving the lid off the toothpaste,
And a half cold tea on the side.
Not screwing the lid of the jam jar down,
Or leaving the bread untied.

The towel hung over the edge of the bath,
Your socks tossed onto the floor.
The teaspoon left on the kitchen sink,
Or never closing a drawer!

And constantly losing your glasses,
And tripping over your shoes.
And forgetting at night to switch off the light,
Or snoozing in front of the news.

These little things used to annoy me,
But I'll miss them now everyday.
The things that used to bother me so,
I wish I could make them all stay.

I loved you so much despite all these things,
So silly they'd drive me mad.
The jobs not begun or the ones half done,
Without them will leave me sad.

So, I'll make sure the lid's off the toothpaste,
And a half cold tea on the side.
These things will be a reminder of you,
And live in my heart with pride.

The Coachman
In memory of Brian

We did a private memorial service for a gentleman who drove coaches for a living. He absolutely loved his work and took groups all over Australia with his wife by his side. A beautiful family and one we became very close to whilst we organised his service. He was a simple man who enjoyed the simple things in life. A meticulous planner who took joy in everything he did.

This poem would suit a coach driver or someone who enjoyed travelling holidays. It would be difficult to change the gender for this poem although not impossible.

Tips to Customise

The gender of this poem can be changed from Male to Female.

Verse Six can be changed to:

'A wife, sister, a mother too, their respect she did so earn.
A Grandma (Nana) with a gentle heart, she loved each one in turn.'

The Coachman

by Kate Armon and Craig Smith

As the sun comes up on dusty ground, new light to shine the way.
The Coachman stands with keys in hand, preparing for the day.

The tyres checked, the windows clean, the coach so gleaming white.
He helped the patrons in his charge and showed them all the sights.

From North to South, and East to West, they travelled this vast red land.
Across the country girt by sea, two soulmates hand in hand.

And when the driving day was done, some time to rest his head.
The Coachman, he loved nothing more than a tale and a glass of red.

For the Coachman was a simple man, his heart so full of love.
Always there, advice to share, an angel from above.

A husband, brother, a father too, their respect he did so earn.
A Grandad with a gentle heart, he loved each one in turn.

A tower of strength to one and all, he'd give a gentle smile.
A little wink and a wise word too, he would go the extra mile.

The driver's seat is empty now, the ignition key is missing.
The family left with smiles and tears, and years of reminiscing.

So, when the sun sets on your final tour, fear not and don't dismay.
You'll be received with a helping hand, for the Coachman's on his way.

The Sun is Up
In memory of Gayle

This poem has a special place in our hearts, as it was the first poem we wrote for a family. Sadly, so many of the families we help lose a loved one to cancer and this family had lost a beautiful wife and mother to this terrible disease. They were lost in grief and their story truly touched our souls.

As we sat with them, we talked about suitable poems. There was just nothing that truly captured the spirit of this beautiful woman and what was important in her life. Before we knew what we were doing, we had told the family we would write a poem. Although the 'The Sun is Up' is simplistic in nature we are still proud of it, as it was our first attempt at creating bespoke poetry for our families.

Tips to Customise

The location referenced in Verse One can be changed to suit.

To change the gender of the poem from female to male, verse one can be changed to:

> *The sun's just up in Josephville,*
> *When this Gentleman/man starts to rise,*
> *With horses, chooks and goats to feed*
> *He rubs his weary eyes.*

Verses Five and Six can be changed to:

> *Now a Father and a hubby*
> *His family brought such joys*
> *He nurtured, loved and brought them up*
> *So proud of his two boys.*

> *What will we do now that he's not here,*
> *To laugh with us each day,*
> *"We'll carry on and do our best"*
> *Is what our Dad would say.*

The remainder of the poem *'her'* can be swapped for *'he'*

The Sun is Up

by Kate Armon and Craig Smith

The sun's just up in Josephville, when this lady starts to rise,
With horses, chooks and goats to feed, she rubs her weary eyes.

They see her coming it's all excitement, they 'neigh' and shake their manes
Tenderly she brushes them, despite her searing pain.

Fluffy kittens and baby lambs, her favourite time for living,
The Spring with all its newborn life, a time for real thanksgiving.

In her childhood how she loved to ride, and show her little horses,
With rosettes, wins and trophies, oh, so many courses.

Now a Mother and a wife, her family brought such joys.
She nurtured, loved and brought them up, so proud of her two boys.

What will we do now that she's not here, to laugh with us each day,
"We'll carry on and do our best", is what our Mum would say.

The Collector
In memory of George

We often ask our families, how would they describe their loved one in a few words. When we asked this family that question, the eldest daughter jumped right in and described her father to us as a 'Collector'. The other daughters all agreed. We had never heard anyone being described in such a way, so we asked them to clarify. They did not mean a collector of inanimate objects or worthless possessions; their father was a collector of people, experiences and life.

We thought this was a beautiful way to describe someone, and all by itself told a beautiful story. Because in its essence it meant that he cared deeply for those around him and the experiences that made up his, sometimes complicated but beautiful life.

Tips to Customise

The gender of the poem can easily be changed from Male to Female.

Verse Two is very specific to the gentleman we wrote this for and can therefore be omitted if necessary.

Verse Five can use the alternative of:
> *A loving mum, a storyteller,*
> *A great protector too.*
> *With loyalty beyond repair,*
> *She was always there for you.*

'Mum' can be swapped for *'Mom'* as per the global region.

The Collector

by Kate Armon and Craig Smith

Our Father was a Collector,
Of many wonderful things.
Of people, memories, experiences,
And all that happiness brings.

A croc catcher, a prison guard,
And footy in PNG.
From trading sheep, and railway time,
The challenge was the key.

Of all the towns he'd been to,
The places far and wide.
Through the different versions of his life,
His children were his pride.

If you were bored, or wanted a chat,
He was right there on the spot.
Cheer you up with just one word,
He loved to stir the pot.

A larrikin, a storyteller,
A hunter-gatherer too.
With loyalty beyond repair,
He was always there for you.

There's one less road to travel now,
And one less face to know.
But rest assured on your next step,
Our love's with you as you go.

Yes, our father was a Collector,
A Collector of many things.
Thank you, Dad, for all you've done,
And all that your love brings.

Keep the Tinnies Cold

In memory of Bob

This poem came from a request from this gentleman's family to 'give him something funny to send him on his way.' He had an extremely dry and wicked sense of humour in life, and would often joke with his children that they were only hanging around to get his money!

It is a poem that can certainly only be used for someone who had a real dry sense of humour; someone who wanted to go out with a bang and give everyone a good laugh.

The term *'bugger me'* is a very Australian (and English) one and for the benefit of those in other countries who don't understand its context, it means, 'I'll be damned!' or something along a similar vein.

Likewise the term *'Tinnie'* is Australian slang for Beer Can.

Tips to Customise

For overseas readers, the first line can be changed to:

'Well, I'll be, this is rough,'

The word 'tinnies' in the second last line can be altered to:
'Brewski's' or simply *'Beers'*.

Keep the Tinnies Cold.

by Kate Armon and Craig Smith

Well, bugger me, this is rough,
It appears that I've dropped dead!
No doubt there must be a lot of questions,
Running through your heads.

Like who gets the car, or even the house?
And what about the cash?
I'm sure your all thinking, this old bastard's
Got a secret stash!

Well, here's the news, so gather round
You Vulture's one and all.
There's nothing there, I spent the lot,
And had myself a ball!

Yes, life was good, I lived it well,
And left without regrets.
And now the joke's on you, my friends,
I've left you all my debts!

But now's the time to tell you all,
It's not hard for me to say.
I love you lots, my family
And I'll miss you every day.

So, carry on 'til your journey's done,
Don't weep or shed a tear.
Just know I'll keep the tinnies cold,
For when you all get here.

The Cyclone
In memory of Blake

This poem was written for a young man who, sadly, took his own life. Suicide comes as a shock to everyone, and for this family even more so, as this young man was, on the surface, bright and energetic, with a full life ahead of him.

His mother had three children; she described them to us as, "Thunder, Lightning and Cyclone". This young man was The Cyclone.

Tips to Customise

This poem doesn't refer to a specific gender and can be used for any family who has been touched by a great loss.

The Cyclone

by Kate Armon and Craig Smith

You came and blew across our path,
A raindrop on my face.
I wipe my cheek, I close my eyes,
A tear left in its place.

At first a breeze and then a gale,
We watched you grow and grow.
The cyclone's call, it gathered speed,
Your life it did not slow.

Through wind and gale, you showed no fear,
A bough that bends not breaks.
Your strength and courage unrestrained,
Oh, how our hearts do ache.

But in amongst the storms that rage,
The darkness and the light.
A central calm, a peace within,
A pleasant, wondrous sight.

But now the storm has gone away,
A path is left behind.
Of love, of laughs, of broken dreams,
Imprinted in our minds.

The cyclone whistled through our lives,
And passed in just a beat.
Don't mourn the winds, for they'll return,
When once again we meet.

My Friend

One of the strongest relationships you can have with a person is as a friend. There is a saying, 'Friends are the family we choose'. No truer word was ever spoken.

Often friendship loss is overlooked at funerals, because of the more direct relationships involved. We honour the role of friendships in our lives with this poem.

Tips to Customise

Verse Three can be changed from Male to Female gender.
ie: *man to woman*

My Friend

by Kate Armon and Craig Smith

You've been my friend for many a year,
We've shared our lives, always been near,
Now you've gone I feel great fear,
That I can't live without you here.

How will I pass each hour away?
Without you always in my day,
If only death could be kept at bay,
And instead, together we could stay.

They say, He only picks the best,
To go early to eternal rest,
To choose a man so full of zest,
With all the life that you possessed.

Life must proceed, it must go on,
However, much it feels so wrong,
I will continue to sing your song,
Till at last, I too am gone.

Then once more we'll be together
Two best friends, birds of a feather,
A friendship made to stand all weather,
And one that death cannot untether.

So, see you soon, my beautiful friend,
And think of all the time we'll spend,
Go with my love, which I now send,
Until we meet in Heaven again.

Give Me Back My Boots and Saddle
In memory of Raymond

This poem was written for a gentleman who spent a large part of his younger years working as a Jackaroo. An avid horse rider all the way into his senior years, the bush was a part of his life, and he never went anywhere without his hat.

When we met with the family, his wife showed us his boots and saddle which sat, still polished, in the corner of his garage, underneath framed posters of great old western films like *The Magnificent Seven* and *The Searchers*. That gave us the inspiration for this poem.

Tips to Customise

If the person mustered cattle only, then Verse Two, Line Three can be changed to read;

> *'twelve hundred head of sturdy beast.'*

Or any such relevant number.

The word *'Jackaroo'* could be changed to *'Jillaroo'*, if relevant. Likewise, this word could be changed to *'Stockmen'* or *'Ringers'* if appropriate.

'Billy' (kettle) and *'Swag'* (sleeping bag) are very Australian terms, so Verse One, Line Three can be changed to:
> *'Pack the pot and the bedroll too'*

An alternative to Verse Two, Line Two is;
> *'Along the open plains'*

Give Me Back My Boots and Saddle

by Craig Smith and Kate Armon

Give me back my boots and saddle,
Grab the hat down from the hook.
Pack the billy and roll the swag
And throw in a damn good book.

The days are long of drought and heat,
Along the prairies plain.
Twelve hundred head of golden fleece,
Without a drop of rain.

With mouths a dry and hands a cracked,
It's a long and tiring wait,
To see the drove now come to pass
And make the station gate.

Across the breezes of the west,
You'll hear the stockwhips crack
Where the Jackaroos and hands all sing,
To the prairies calling back.

So, give me back my boots and saddle,
And point me t'wards the west.
For one last ride to beat 'em all,
Wish me all the best.

And the Answer is...

In memory of Norm

No two funerals are the same. Occasionally we get asked to write comical poems for funerals and memorial services. *The Answer Is* came from a conversation with a family friend about what he would like to say at his brother's funeral.

Norm was a man with a very naughty sense of humour, but while his brother felt that the funeral needed to reflect this, he was worried that anything funny might be taken out of context and be seen as inappropriate. We assured him that the guests were all people that Norm knew, so they knew of his sharp sense of humour and that Norm himself wouldn't want the day to be a dour event, he'd want people to have a laugh at his expense.

We wrote the poem from the perspective of Norm's brother.

...no one walked out in offence.

Tips to Customise

This poem is of a more generic nature and, as such, has no customisation options.

And the Answer Is...

by Craig Smith and Kate Armon

So long, my friend, I say goodbye
And bid you a fond farewell.
I hope the good deeds you've done in life
Stop you from going to Hell!

I hear it's pretty rough down there
With debauchery and more.
But knowing you, it's what you'd want,
You'd beg and ask for more!

I reckon though, that there is a chance,
With odds of five to seven.
That you will make it all the way
To the fluffy clouds of Heaven.

You'd have to get through Peter first,
At the gates of Gold and Pearl.
But then again, you don't do heights,
You'd probably want to hurl!

So, what's that answer, fluffy clouds
Or the fiery pits of dread?
I bet you'll probably stay right here
And haunt us all instead!

The Mechanic
In memory of Brian

This poem was written for a man who raced the Speedway circuit in his younger days. He was a tinkerer, and loved anything to do with engines and cars. He could be found happily working in his shed most days, contented in life as long as his cars and precious family were near to him.

There are not too many poems out there about mechanics. It was an enjoyable poem to write, and the family loved it as they felt it perfectly reflected their man, 'Myers'.

Tips to Customise

The second verse can be changed to:

With hands precise he laid the plans,
With tools he lit the fire.
To build an engine full of love,
A man they all admire.

Verse 5 was very specific to the family and can be omitted.

In the final verse the name *'Myers'* can be changed to suit.
If required, this poem can be changed to reflect a woman who enjoys mechanics.

The Mechanic

by Kate Armon and Craig Smith

'Twas in the shed I heard the sounds
Of engines fast and loud.
The spark of fuel, the smell of oil,
And a man who stood so proud.

With hands precise he laid the plans,
With tools he lit the fires.
To build an engine full of love,
The man they all called Myers

A Spanner here, a Wrench in there,
He tinkered as he toiled.
The Mechanic worked both day and night,
To keep his engine oiled.

And when a part came tumbling down,
A gentle hand did lay.
"We'll brush you off and fix you up,
To race another day."

And then one day a bike came by,
On this you'll soon be screamin'!
A thousand bucks for that old thing?
Three-fifty or tell him he's dreamin'!

The engine roar is silenced now,
The ignition key is missing.
The family left with smiles and tears,
And years of reminiscing.

So, when you hear the Speedway sounds,
Just give a little grin.
And send a nod as the man called Myers,
Comes racing for the win.

The Chippy
In memory of Trevor

This is one of our more heavily personalised poems. This man was a wonderful father and husband with a passion for carpentry. We often say at funerals that one of the saddest parts of our job is that we are only ever introduced to people in death and not in life. This is especially true of this gentleman; he was such an interesting man with so many different facets to his life. Poetry is our way of feeling connected to the person who has passed away and to the family who is left behind.

Tips to Customise

In Verse One, Line One, the location *'Otaki'* can be changed to suit.

In Verse Five, Line One, *'X's'* refers to an Australian beer, XXXX (Four X). This verse can be changed to something more generic:
'He loved a good beer and he'd give the all clear,
when it came to the end of the day'

In Verse Six, Line One, *'young girls'* can be changed to *'young boys'*

Verse Eight, Line Four *'Trev'll'*, short for *Trev will*, can be changed to another name.

The Chippy

by Kate Armon and Craig Smith

In Otaki one day a child came their way,
The parents were loving young folks.
The fourth one of six, he entered the mix,
They shared all their dreams and their hopes.

They watched the boy grow, and in time he showed
His passion for wood and the tools.
This handsome young fox as strong as an ox,
He surely was nobody's fool.

A Chippy was he, and a good one you see,
His father gave him his first start.
This cheeky young bloke who loved a good joke,
Turned work into a bloody fine art.

The time it did come for a house to be done,
To give shelter to all of his clan.
In three months, it grew from nothing to new,
And out of the shed they all ran.

The X's times four was his beer evermore,
He enjoyed at the end of the day.
He felt his bones creak 'cause he worked all the week,
When the kids said, "Dad come out and play!"

So, when his young girls would call, he had time for them all,
No matter how worn out and tired.
He played a good horsey, didn't tolerate naughty,
And for this they all so admired.

His thing became walking and while they were talking,
They took to the long-distance track.
While shooting the breeze he said of the trees,
"I can talk and they don't answer back!"

So, let the sadness abstain and the memories remain,
For forever we'll have all the tales.
But no doubt somewhere ol' Trev'll be there,
And he'll be still bangin' in nails.

Flying High
In memory of John

This was a poem we wanted to write within a few minutes of meeting this wonderful family.   John was such an interesting character and we knew straight away that we would need a very special poem for this man.

John joined the Royal Australian Air Force, and was the Australian champion parachutist for two years in a row, he then formed a parachute club in his local area. He had done over 6,000 jumps from every type of plane you can imagine!

We felt very privileged as we sat with the family to look through the most wonderful photograph albums of all his amazing achievements.

Tips to Customise

The religious reference in Verse Six can be changed to something more generic such as:

eg: *On Golden wings I fly,*

Flying High

by Kate Armon and Craig Smith

Flying high above the clouds,
My adrenaline starts to flow,
The plane doors open, I feel the wind,
It's time for me to go.

A familiar rush as I start to fall,
Like a soaring bird in flight,
I see the land way below,
A truly magnificent sight.

My chute pulls open I see it bloom
Then it starts to tug,
The straps they tighten all around me,
Just like an old friend's hug.

The ground now approaches I see it clearly,
My heart beats oh so fast,
As my feet touch the earth I wish so dearly,
That this feeling could always last.

Don't lose a tear, don't weep for me,
Your heads should not be bowed.
For this where I wish to be,
Right here, amongst the clouds.

For now, my soul has been set free,
On Angels wings I fly,
At one with the world, I see it all,
As I say my last goodbye.

Turn Out the Light

The need to protect loved ones is something that can be described as 'primal'. The sense of comfort in making sure that everyone is safe and warm is one of the driving motivations behind love for others.

This poem tries to encapsulate that feeling. Told from the perspective of the departed, it relays the wish to make sure that those left behind remain protected from harm, whilst keeping their memory alive within their hearts and minds.

Tips to Customise

Verse Three, Line One can be changed to *'coffee'*.

You may need to change your inflection on either the word *'coffee'* or on the word *'me'* in the next line.

Turn Out the Light

by Craig Smith and Kate Armon

When I am gone and you're still here,
Don't be afraid, don't live with fear.
Lock the doors, keep the windows tight,
And don't forget to turn out the light.

Just be sure to keep the place,
Safe and well from harm's embrace.
So, check the halls and every room,
Don't let our house be filled with gloom.

Let the kettle boil and make the tea,
And set an extra place for me.
Just sit and we can chat all day,
And pretend I didn't go away.

Don't sit upon the porch and stare,
Or be alone without me there.
For in my heart, you'll always dwell,
With mine in yours, you're safe and well.

So, when I'm gone and you remain,
Don't be afraid, don't cry in vain.
My love will keep you safe at night,
Each time that you turn out the light.

A Beautiful Journey

In memory of Selina

We spent the most idyllic afternoon with this inspiring woman's son. He was an extraordinary individual who had chosen to live off the grid in a beautiful but simple home, surrounded by water, trees and wildlife. Our mobiles wouldn't work and there wasn't a TV or radio to be seen anywhere. It was an incredibly peaceful meeting, we didn't want to leave!

As we sat there we felt every emotion in its purest and most real form. We felt the connection to nature and our surroundings that is so often lost in this busy world of ours. *'A Beautiful Journey'* was the story of this woman's life.

Tips to Customise

The gender can be changed easily from Female to Male.

A Beautiful Journey

by Kate Armon and Craig Smith

A beautiful journey,
She has traveled so far,
Under the rage of the sun,
And by many a star.

A childhood of freedom,
Living life from the land,
A precious gift given,
To their little hands.

A love of the red land,
With its beauty and richness,
She taught them to live,
From its abundance and freshness.

Her soul mate appeared,
Her heart skipped along,
They set forth together,
A familiar old song.

Now it was their journey,
Her love by her side,
The open road ahead of them,
Oh, what a ride.

A new sense of purpose,
Her life so renewed,
Of childlike wonder,
For the world that they viewed.

The heart of a Mother,
Of love and acceptance,
She will be so missed,
In this act of remembrance.

When the breezes all blow,
And the birds start to sing,
Just think of her here,
A part of all things.

Our Family Tree

In memory of Jon

It is a wonderful thing when you come across a family that have an unbreakable bond. They sort out their differences and are stronger for them. They take time in their days to check on each other. It's not a chore, they do it because they want to and because their love for each other is so strong.

The loss of an anchor like this in a family is heartbreaking, because the family is truly symbiotic, they exist within each others lives, offering support and care for each other in a way that supports everyone equally. As they move forward it will be that strength that will eventually help them to heal.

Tips to Customise

This poem is of a more generic nature and, as such, has no customisation options.

Our Family Tree

by Kate Armon and Craig Smith

Our family tree tells the story
Of foundations strong and true.
A tapestry of many chapters,
The start of ours was you.

Rings of the tree show wisdom and age,
Each line a moment shared.
Circles of life that encompass us all
And show how much we cared.

But the winds of time began to blow
And bend our family tree.
For as much we tried, we couldn't hide
What the seasons could foresee.

A time without you near us,
Or a day without you here.
Your softest touch, a gentle smile
Your presence always near.

And now our tree feels broken,
With branches bruised and torn.
A hollow space where you once were
With fallen leaves to mourn.

Our house once echoed laughter,
If only walls could speak.
Fond memories, now lost to time,
A tear runs down my cheek.

But future hearts will hear your name.
We'll speak of it with grace,
A legacy we shan't forget,
Though you're lost from our embrace.

Yes, our family tree continues on
With buds that spring anew.
Rest now your journeys at its end,
Our love, it goes with you.

Our Mother

In memory of all Mothers

We have dedicated this poem to all Mothers who have left an indelible mark on our lives.

These amazing women who give up so much in their own lives, to be women of strength in the lives of others. Who give us support and love when we need it and who always put their children first. When these women leave our lives a hole is left that can never be filled, a piece of heart goes with them and never returns.

Tips to Customise

This poem is of a more generic nature and, as such, has no customisation options.

Our Mother

by Kate Armon and Craig Smith

Our Mother had a gentle heart, and now our lives are torn apart,
How do we journey on without her wisdom by our side?
Always there and always ready, her voice was calm, her advice was steady,
The road it seems so awfully empty without her as our guide.

From our first steps that each we took, to reading to us from a book,
Her caring ways, the love she showed, filled our lives with joy.
She wore her love upon her sleeve, it wasn't hard for us to believe,
We were her life, the centre of it, she loved us more than life itself.

She always nurtured and never scolded, her love for us too enfolded,
No matter how we acted, she was always there for us.
We certainly caused her much heartache, with all our failings and mistakes,
But never did she falter in the love she gave to us.

Mum, we miss you in our lives, we promise each of us will strive,
To live a life, you would be proud of, one of courage and of love.
We will learn from your good ways, teach our own till the end of days,
That life is precious and full of joy and not a day should be wasted.

A mother's love unending, a family story that's transcending
All the things you taught us; we will remember for all of time
You taught us to be good and true, face our worries and see them through,
Your loss is the hardest thing we've faced but this too we will do with grace.

How will we live and carry on, without you here now you have gone?
We'll take each day as it comes, and keep you in our heart.
Your work on earth is now done, you've finished the race and now you've won,
One day we'll meet again and then once more we'll never part.

Man's Best Friend

In memory of Millie

A couple of years ago Dad's dog Millie had to be put to sleep. She was a boisterous young Labrador, full of life and everyone who met her, loved her. We all considered her our dog, even though she was most loyal to Dad.

In the middle of the night we had a phone call from Dad asking us to drive them to the vet with Millie, as she wasn't well. The vet told us there was nothing they could do and our beautiful Millie needed to be put to sleep. It was devastating.

It's so easy to gloss over the loss of a family pet but research shows that grieving the death of our pets can be just as painful, if not more than grieving the loss of a family member or friend. For some, our dogs are the centre of our world.

Tips to Customise

Verse One, Line One, the word *'leash'* can be interchanged for *'lead'*.

To change Verse Two, Lines Three and Four from Male to Female, use the following:

> *'Your big brown eyes, sorrowful and glum,*
> *As you said goodbye to your human Mum.'*

or for US readers:

> *'Your big brown eyes, full of sorrow and calm,*
> *As you said goodbye to your human Mom.'*

If preferred, the last line in Verse Seven can be changed to:

> *'My friend and my pal, I'll see you one day.'*

Man's Best Friend

By Kate Armon & Craig Smith

Your bed lay empty, your leash hangs still,
My chair has a space that you used to fill,
How do I measure the void that you leave?
And will people realise that I need to grieve?

For you were my family, you were my friend,
You loved unconditionally right to the end,
Your big brown eyes, sorrowful and sad,
As you said goodbye to your human Dad.

I'll miss the wet licks that woke me at dawn,
As you waited with angst as I woke with a yawn,
Busily nudging me up with your nose,
Hoping I'd dress and get into some clothes.

Our lovely walks through bushes and tracks,
You loved the adventure, the sun on our backs,
We wandered for miles, just you and me,
Before collapsing at home with a nice cup of tea.

I don't want to walk without you by my side,
The park seems so empty, I just want to hide,
Just one set of footsteps, the journey is hard,
I can no longer hear your bark in the yard.

I picked up your toys to put them away,
But I know I'm not ready, I want you to stay,
Just a day or an hour, together to spend,
A lifetime again, and never to end.

So, wait for me friend, and sit by the chair,
And keep the place warm for when I get there.
Then we can go walking and together we'll play,
My buddy, my pal I'll see you one day.

Part 2

BLESSINGS

What is a Blessing?

A blessing or a benediction is usually spoken at the end of a service. The term, *'benediction'* is usually associated with a religious service, while the more generic *'blessing'* is more commonly used for a non-religious or secular service.

A blessing is not a necessary part of a modern funeral service; however, many families like to have one said to *'bless'* their loved one on their next journey. And so, a blessing can take many forms, such as the traditional *Irish Blessing* or the popular Native American or *Apache Grief Blessing*, both very beautiful.

While modern funerals are becoming less 'heavy', and more of a celebration of life, humorous blessings have become very popular, in accordance with the particular sense of humour of the deceased. Light-hearted and humorous blessings related to a loved one's passions, hobbies or occupation are often a way to end a service on an uplifting note, but again – this should be treated in accordance with the family's wishes and the sense of humour of their loved one. Not all blessings of this nature will be appropriate.

Over the years, we have written a number of humorous blessings for many different hobbies and occupations, as well as some more sentiment based blessings with an uplifting tone.

Sentiment Blessings

The Journey Blessing

May your journey be free from trouble
May your dreams set forth across the sky
May your spirit soar on the winds that guide you
And the sunlight lift you on high
And until next we met
May you be eternally blessed by all who loved you

The Restful Blessing

As you journey on, I hope there'll be
Eternal sunshine and a shady tree.
Somewhere to rest from life's worry
A place of peace, where there is no hurry

The Legacy Blessing

May your stories be told through the valleys of time,
May your songs be sung with passionate spirit.
May your memories be cherished by all who knew you,
And may peace fall upon those in your heart.

The Peace Blessing

May the winds of time carry your name softly through the ages
May your spark ignite the passion in others to thrive
May the peace of your being live on in everyone's hearts
And may your memory bring comfort to those who remain.

The Light Blessing

May light shine upon the sadness in your heart
May the echoes of love remain true
May your memories set a smile upon your face
And bring everlasting peace to you

The Farewell Blessing

May the sun always come out to greet you.
May the light of love always shine upon your face
May peace fall upon those in your heart
And until we are reunited
May God keep you safe in His care.

The Actor's Blessing

May you always be centre stage,
May your script be firmly in your mind,
May standing ovations greet you warmly,
As your song begins to play,
And until the curtain falls for me,
Break a leg as you start your next show.

Humorous Blessings

The Angler's Blessing

May your sinker stay sunk and your flies remain true.
May your bobbers stay bobbing out there on the blue.

May your chum always float and your catch always stay.
And may you long tell the tale of the one that got away.

May the fish always nibble on the bait that you choose.
May your rod keep its flex and your lines never lose.

May your tackle never lose its lustre and sheen.
And may your hook remain sharp and know where it's been!

Mountain Biker's Blessing

May your brakes never fail,
May your legs never ache.
And as you ride along the trail,
May your chain never break!

May you always long to train,
May your paths be ever free.
And until we meet again,
Keep pedalling for me.

The Mechanic's Blessing

May your wrench never tumble
May your iron never tire
May your sockets never stumble
And your engine not misfire

Keep the oil from the water
And the water from the fuel
May your engine not get hotter
And your gaskets all stay cool

May your plugs always spark
Your transmission never slip.
May your timings hit their mark
And your hose never drip.

The Handyman's Blessing

May your hammer never miss and your socket never slip
May your saws remain sharp and your vice always grip

May the walls you erect always stay plumb and true
And may the overalls you wear stay faithful to you.

The Knitters Blessing

May your needles never break,
May your wool never tangle,
May you have lots of things to make,
And your yarn always dangle.

May you never drop a stitch,
Of purl, herringbone or knit,
May your work never hit a hitch,
And your jumpers always fit.

And until we meet again,
Keep knitting just for me.

Part 3

HAIKUS

What is a Haiku?

Sometimes it's hard to find little phrases or words that fit someone completely as part of an introduction or a bigger speech. We often like to start our services with a quote or a short 'one verse' poem. Something that helps tie in a theme.

There are many different types of poetry. Haiku is a beautiful form of poetry, originating in Japan, that is non-rhyming, and uses only three lines. It focuses on a theme designed to evoke an emotionally charged response in only seventeen syllables. The first line has five syllables, the second has seven and the last line has five. It celebrates the juxtaposition between the theme and the self.

Traditional Japanese Haikus focus on nature themes, however modern English Haikus may focus on other themes.

A Haiku is perfect for that little 'breaker' in a service, designed to bridge the gap between one topic and another. For example, between an introduction and a eulogy, or between words of comfort and a committal.

Hopefully, you may find a place one or more of these in your services.

Calling out your name
I hear the still of the night
Answer in silence.

Still trapped by my heart
I feel the ground beneath me
Give way to my tears.

Clouds fall over me,
Dark tears that rinse my soul clean
And bathe me in light.

Your memory sleeps
On the pillow next to me,
My dreams of you wake.

Waking without you
Feels like the long emptiness
That only sleep brings.

Hang not your head low
For light and song fill my soul.
I am now at peace.

You are in my thoughts.
Even if you're far away,
You are in my heart.

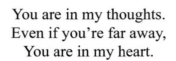

Beginning with life,
Love binds our souls together
Even when apart.

My heart feels so bruised
Without you here to hold me.
Life will cease to be.

Like the flowing tide,
My lonely soul rips and falls
Now you are not here.

I watch the eagle
Soar above the endless clouds,
I hope you are there.

My mind is empty,
My heart is broken in two.
Why did you leave me?

Lost without you here.
When will my tears stop falling,
My heart is so numb.

My heart feels empty
Without you here by my side
To guide me safely.

Memories of you
Live on in my lonely heart,
Keeping me alive.